"In Kerri French's *Every Room in the Body*, we lear___ ly of the
speaker's high-risk pregnanc___ ___orn but
maybe not alive' and, by

The waiting was like a da
inside me, a gunshot fired
across a clear field

Each line in this fine book is a depth change packed full of images
that are at once gorgeous and devastating. Each poem ratchets the
tension higher. We tiptoe through this minefield of 'will be/ born
but maybe not' with held breath and hope growing in our guts for
what surely 'will be.'"

—SARAH FRELIGH, AUTHOR OF *Sad Math*

"Kerri French's *Every Room in the Body* is an eloquent story of sys-
tems, a blueprint of two lives perilously carried to term. As rooms in
this house take shape, the body is rearranged impossibly. It becomes
a 'captor' 'refusing to let' mother and daughter 'go.' Inside these fluid
poems—part fantasy, part allegory, part cautionary tale—French
relates the experience of this life to 'a gunshot fired/ across a clear
field.' As with Dickinson's 'Loaded Gun,' an eerie peace finally pre-
vails. In the cool afterbirth of French's words, readers will find them-
selves dazed under the transformative power of this new origin story."

—SANDRA MARCHETTI, AUTHOR OF *Confluence*

EVERY ROOM
IN THE BODY

POEMS | KERRI FRENCH

MOON CITY PRESS

For Imogen and Theodore

MOON CITY PRESS
Department of English
Missouri State University
901 South National Avenue
Springfield, Missouri 65897

The stories contained herein are works of fiction. All incidents, situations, institutions, governments, and people are fictional, and any similarity to characters or persons living or dead is strictly coincidental.

First Edition
Copyright © 2017 by Kerri French
All rights reserved.
Published by Moon City Press, Springfield, Missouri, USA, in 2017.

Library of Congress Cataloging-in-Publication Data

French, Kerri
Every room in the body: poems/Kerri French, 1981–

2017945939

Further Library of Congress information is available upon request.

ISBN-10: 0-913785-94-6
ISBN-13: 978-0-913785-94-2

Cover and interior illustrated and designed by Charli Barnes

Edited by Lanette Cadle & Karen Craigo
Text copyedited by Karen Craigo

Manufactured in the United States of America.

www.mooncitypress.com

ACKNOWLEDGEMENTS

Grateful acknowledgement is made to the editors of the publications in which these poems first appeared, sometimes in slightly different versions or with different titles:

Barrelhouse Magazine: "In Doorways, Every Sign"
Barrow Street: "Elegy for the House"
BOAAT: "To Bring Milk Anyway"
Copper Nickel: "The Doctor Asks Me to Describe the Pain"
Fugue: "I Dreamed I Called Him—No, Wait, I Did"
HOUSEGUEST Magazine: "34 Weeks," "Perigee," and "Years From Now, I Remember Our Vacation"
The Journal: "The Funeral Year"
LUMINA: "Dear Hands,"
Magma Poetry: "Libraries"
Moon City Review: "32 Weeks"
Nashville Review: "The Doctor Asks Me When the Pain Began"
Painted Bride Quarterly: "Cherry Hill"
PANK: "Daytime Television, Late-Night Sex," and "Meshes of the Afternoon"
Sou'wester: "Cut"
storySouth: "Should We Need to Escape"
Tinderbox Poetry Journal: "Blue Feathers"
Waccamaw: "Battle Forest" and "Letting the Body Decide"
Washington Square Review: "Say the Eels Return"

Several of these poems also appear in a chapbook, *Instruments of Summer* (Dancing Girl Press, 2013).

"Apogee" was published in *All We Can Hold* (Sage Hill Press, 2016).

"27 Weeks" was featured on the *All We Can Hold* website.

"Dear Hands," was reprinted in *The Southern Poetry Anthology, Volume 5: Georgia* (Texas Review Press, 2012).

"Elegy for the House" was reprinted online in *Redux*.

"I Go Back to the Doll Hospital" was published in *The Doll Collection* (Terrapin Books, 2016).

"In Doorways, Every Sign" was reprinted in *Click of Time: Reflections of the Digital Age* (Anglia Ruskin University, 2010).

"Meshes of the Afternoon" was reprinted in *Crab Creek Review*.

Thank you to my teachers and mentors at the University of North Carolina at Chapel Hill, the University of North Carolina at Greensboro, and Boston University, especially Alan Shapiro, A. Van Jordan, Stuart Dischell, Linda Gregg, and Julia Johnson. For their support and encouragement, I am indebted to the Writers' Room of Boston, ICP Support, and the wonderful Nashville and Murfreesboro writing communities.

I would also like to thank Stephanie Rogers, Sarah Sweeney, Jennifer Givhan, Gabrielle Calvocoressi, Lauren Moseley, and especially Jennifer K. Sweeney for their feedback and encouragement on drafts of this manuscript. Thanks also to Christina Stoddard, whose advice steered this book towards becoming a book.

Many thanks to Charli Barnes for the beautiful cover, and my deepest gratitude to Lanette Cadle, Michael Czyzniejewski, and everyone at Moon City Press for making this book possible.

Most of all, thank you to my parents for their unconditional love and support, and more than thanks to my husband, David Nelson, and our children, Immy and Theo, for each and every day together.

Dwelling 1
   Elegy For a Forgotten Fairytale 3
   Feather, Nest, House, Home 5
   24 Weeks 6
   Or Just a River 7
   Cut 8
   In Which I Play the Part of Myself 9
   Diagnosis 10
   The Doctor Asks Me When the Pain Began 12
   Perigee 14
   After the Diagnosis, No One Calls 15
   I Go Back to the Doll Hospital 16
   Battle Forest 17
   27 Weeks 18
   We Painted Names Across Floorboards 19
   Elegy for the House 20
   So I'll See You Next Wednesday 21

Occupancy 23
   Residence 25
   I Dreamed I Called Him — No, Wait, I Did 26
   Roof 27
   Separation, Sometimes 28
   The Doctor Asks Me to Describe the Pain 29
   Apogee 30
   Should We Need to Escape 32
   Daytime Television, Late-Night Sex 34
   In Doorways, Every Sign 36
   The Doctor Asks Me to Recall My Dream 37
   Meshes of the Afternoon 38
   Dear Hands, ... 40
   Blue Feathers 41

Domicile 43

   The Funeral Year 45

   Libraries 46

   Each Morning, I Wake Reaching 47

   32 Weeks 48

   Years From Now, I Remember Our Vacation 49

   34 Weeks 50

   The Doctor Asks Me to Imagine My Baby Alive 51

   In My Dream, I Always Remember the Names of Trees 52

   36 Weeks 53

   Letting the Body Decide 54

   Say the Eels Return 55

   To Bring Milk Anyway 56

   An Archaeology 57

   Cherry Hill 58

   The Country We Came From 59

   Waterside.. 60

Notes 63

EVERY ROOM
IN THE BODY

POEMS | KERRI FRENCH

MOON CITY PRESS

DWELLING

A knife. The loneliness of a forehead.

I spoke to my reflection in every mirror.

The boat's sail grew and grew.

In the windows, mud covered

every baby whose cries I recognized.

The fortune-teller waved to no

passing ships. Let me begin again.

There was a knife pressed into a shoe.

There was a knife pressed into my stomach.

Doctors scaled the piano until each

patient memorized every note.

Where were the children? Let me

begin before. A girl held a knife.

Her pink dress waved to the fortune-teller.

I turned my back to her reflection.

I ate cake at every funeral.

I held her hand as each boat sank.

FEATHER, NEST, HOUSE, HOME

Because the nest was already in place
when we signed the lease,
I imagined the birds would bring us luck.
Each morning, I saw feathers stirring
as I stood by the sink, the quiet in the courtyard
all that marked one day from the next.
I felt the eyes of the birds follow me
as I moved through the house, empty boxes
stacked in corners, the doctor's advice
to keep still echoing through the rooms.
I didn't know how to tell her my body
continued to move even when my mind
would not, how the birds flew
through the windows each time
I lay down, their small wings fluttering
above the baby's kicks until I grew
too afraid to ask them to leave.

24 WEEKS

Too early, too new, to the west,
        the body fought too long—
    the spleen too large, the liver

pressed too hard, the baby
        too many weeks
            before.

        I packed too many books,
      convinced too many months
in the hospital lay ahead.

Two hours I held my face
        to the floor, too many names
waiting to be crossed from my list.

        Too still to be spoken,
two countries mapped
        beneath my skin.

    One. Two. The lost hours
more than I could count.

        Three days before I knew.

OR JUST A RIVER

Forget the boat, the waves that rose
from one country to the next.
Evening's drift falls closer to shore
and monk seals swim towards sleep.
Forget what was said. Promise me
no words no edge no end or just
a river green orchid no border
new grass no measure no note
no weather no why outside this door.
Forget the face of a rock. Press
your hand to water. Promise no
other. Follow what you cannot stop.

CUT

It was like drawing a map to every room
in the body, the bitter halves of fruit
seared across the stove. It was schooldays,
bathroom stalls, the back garden
under rain. It was the afternoons I slept,
every stone unstacked. Oh, the world
must have seen the initials I laid,
must have heard the steps of my name.
I was a cat scratching at the window.
I was the tree's branch breaking my fall.
I was the way I wanted to be touched.
I traced my hand in chalk. I cut paper
hearts with scissors. I bled. I bruised.
I was the stem of constellations, a pattern
of snowflakes buried between each page.
It was green water calling, the scars
swimming beneath my veins. My back
swore my secrets. Doctors sewed my skin.
I threw bottles against the wall and named
each piece of fallen glass. I followed
the clouds for cover, circled words
splayed like stars across my stomach.
I was a portrait writhing, a fence
crashing, cracked edges in the porcelain.
Even then, I saw my body as a maze.
Lines gave directions. My arms told my age.

IN WHICH I PLAY THE PART OF MYSELF

For a long time, I imagined what others
saw when they looked at me:

a kettle cooling on the counter, limescale
rising to the surface, the dried-out

lawn of summer. No telephone rang,
yet words were always spoken,

my hands a front door I opened and closed
to the empty hallways of other lives.

Sometimes, I kept a steady pace
behind them in the road, the sound

of cars crashing proving like dough
echoing inside an oven.

Always, I swept the glass in piles
beside my ankles. I counted

each piece as it sifted through my hands.
At night, I carved a shore

to sleep on. I mapped the unmade bed
I discovered within myself.

DIAGNOSIS

You're told your baby will be
born but maybe not alive.

Weeks fold in slow motion,
hours stacked around the room.

Decisions hinge on numbers—
heart rates, blood counts,

train schedules, how many
kicks you feel on the ride

to the hospital, how many
pills you swallow in one day.

Doctors speak in melodies
you never remember,

your body an instrument
pulsing notes across machines.

Afraid to fall asleep, you learn
that to wait is to mourn,

each day that passes one more
that you live without a daughter,

a son. The sun rises
and a baby is still inside, so still

you begin to fear the birth,
imagine what it will be

to meet a child who will never be.
You look at children in the station

as if they are yours, their tiny faces
turning to watch the trains depart. *Look,*

the doctor says. *Here, the heart.*
Your mother tells you the story

of your birth over and over.
Your husband recites the research

in his dreams. You learn to wait
is to hope, a different kind of disease.

No one tells you it will be OK.

THE DOCTOR ASKS ME WHEN THE PAIN BEGAN

Three days after my birthday
    while I sat in a theater and watched

        a movie without sound.
            The walk alone in the snow.

The morning I fainted
    in the bathroom, the toilet lid

        cracking against my neck.
        Standing on the evening train

from London, rain dripping
    off bicycles in the aisle. Eighteen,

        drinking vodka on the front lawn.
        Waking from surgery

in the wrong country.
    The day at the beach when we drew

        caskets in the sand
          and buried the empty eggs.

Twenty-three weeks.
    Swallowing six pills each day.

        Slipping on ice.
        The moment at the airport

when I first felt the baby move.
    The first time my eardrum burst on a flight.

        Each goodbye. Each kettle
           scorched on the stove.

The idea of her. The idea
    of not her.

        Ten days after the blood work.
           One week after the biopsy.

Swallowing the stitches.
    The argument across the bridge, mouth

        of a fish brushing the water.
           Forty-three hours awake.

Heat wave in Berlin, the baby
    just an idea circling the nest.

PERIGEE

As the moon appeared, muscle
shifted and the itch set in,
the baby gnawing over bone.
I spoke to the teeth of stars

inked across my arms.
I crawled to the body's edge.
Everyone looked to the sky
as I fell beneath my skin.

Veins wrapped around our limbs
and the baby pulled the clouds
through the window, the room
scratched clean of the dark.

I slept for the first time in days.
I touched the sky with my palms.

AFTER THE DIAGNOSIS, NO ONE CALLS

It was winter and I had not yet
grown tired of crying in my office,

the afternoons shaded
with paper across every window.

The quiet steadied me as regret
once did, no voices left to speak

above the small clicks of keyboard.
I could not recall when the loneliness

began but I felt it the way one hears
a crash before the impact registers.

It moved through my bones
like a memory of sand falling

from my hands.

I GO BACK TO THE DOLL HOSPITAL

After two nights of research, I swallow the pills
not licensed for pregnancy, having decided
to believe the doctor when she says
it's the only way to keep my daughter alive.

I made this choice once as a child
when sending my favorite doll into experimental
transplant surgery: my best friend biting
her lip before pulling one leg off
and trying to replace it with another.

How could we have known the new leg
would never work, its bend no longer
a bend but a snap as it swiftly fell to the floor.

I think now of my friend's face as she tried
all afternoon to connect leg with hip,
her eyes refusing to meet mine.

We thought if we fixed what we could see
the dolls would be happier, the dresses
and shoes easier to slip on—no more
trips to the hospital or casts fashioned
from the last tissues in the box.

BATTLE FOREST

Rain came early: the town's
last train arriving to clouds
sunk like anchors, wind
gripping the neighborhood
as the trees began to fall.
Our bodies were changing
and the roads remained blocked,
the police circling the streets faster
than we could count days after
the boy at school rode off on a bicycle
and was never found.
For weeks, we sat in class
with our heads down, our teacher
unwilling to remove
the nametag from his desk.
At home, our parents watched
the news on mute, pulled
the straps of our helmets tighter.
We stayed by the creek that summer,
wading knee-deep until the leeches
clung to our ankles.
The braver boys stripped
from their clothes and jumped
backwards from the bank,
each girl pretending not to look.

27 WEEKS

When they said the daughter inside me
may pass, I locked the bathroom door
and did not leave the bathtub for a week.
The water rose to my neck
and I allowed myself to swim
in the thoughts of a woman
even loneliness could not climb.
My daughter's body turned
beneath my skin as I counted
cracks in the ceiling, small slivers
pointing to an open window.
I was living in a country where no one
knew me, voices like ripples
I would never reach—the same way
my daughter remained with me
as I slept, her name not yet spoken.

WE PAINTED NAMES ACROSS FLOORBOARDS

We painted names

       across floorboards.

Imagined syllables within ourselves.

Clouds kept the room dark

       and we traced letters in glass.

A daughter emerged

and I sketched

       her face from mine.

Her eyes did not open.

Every window inside

       sealed shut.

We set a place for her at the kitchen table.

We taped dishes together

       and spoke as we slept.

ELEGY FOR THE HOUSE

Ask me which night and I'll tell you the static
always slipped from bedroom to field.
Across the water, the wind stirred a neighbor's voice

and I mistook dust for a circus in moonlight,
counted one hundred bright balloons falling to floor.
Ask me before and I'll tell you I ran through the crops

as if the walls grew wings, slept across a sky
shipped through mountains. The body burned
softer then, each light from inside flashing

the story of what happened. Ask me and I'll tell you
I returned at midnight to find what was lost,
the foundation buried beneath September,

every photograph hidden in grass.

SO I'LL SEE YOU NEXT WEDNESDAY

The dinner turned cold ·   against the window

we sang, we saw   *So I'll see you*   next, I

recall one summer   how I lost   tomorrow

two inches   slept through the week   each afternoon

what was it   we said   our bodies   in April

the fifth day we drove to the mill   the bridge   shook

at our crossing   the words were snow   under

an end of season   the return of morning   a book

he loaned me   the newspaper   wrote a candle

started the building's   fall   how fast

were the words going   he said   goodbye

Wednesday   what is left   of the bedroom

tell me again   how long   did the pages   burn?

OCCUPANCY

RESIDENCE

Here is the woman who made a country
her house, an ocean
sweeping names that rained

for days across fields
behind the cathedral.
Lark. Sparrow. Wren. Dreams

of magnolia burrowing under winter,
weather so small she wondered
whether words would make it through.

Here is the sadness sleeping
beside her, a family of birds nesting
in snow. Here is the bulk of all

that grammar, handfuls of horses running
until they find no edge. Water divides
the leaves she chose for a bed,

an evening train leaving her to swim
the remainder. Here is a map
that multiplies her hunger. Here

is the sound where it all began.
Here is the noise buried behind the river—
a headstone of notes whistling below.

This morning, poems were born from my dying
cat's head. A man in green named each one
as he pulled them from the skull, his hands
filled with the cursive letters I meticulously
practiced one month when I was eight.
From my kitchen to the street, the sun smelled
of black tea, crushed insects whose legs
I couldn't keep apart. I rode an elevator
wearing nearly nothing. It was noon
or maybe later, the heat so tense my shoes
clung to the sidewalk like tiny claws
to skin. Four stories up, my cat gave
a few stiff moans before placing his head
beneath the water bowl. I walked for hours
but never arrived. Hunger stretched to the sky.
My fingers stretched from hunger. Finally,
my horoscope read: If home can be a coast,
an ocean, you're already drowned.
Inside, the man rose like a television character
I once saw grinning in the road.
Let's call this one Heartbreak. I'll like it best,
he said, *because it's most like you.*

ROOF

When the babies appeared
inside the nest, I felt
a sort of envy. Their mouths

opened so perfectly
each time their mother
flew back with worms

from the garden.
I grew tired watching her
and so I began to sleep

when they slept, the mother
with her feathers spread
like a roof over her young.

SEPARATION, SOMETIMES

Sometimes I let the morning decide
and still the night comes out all wrong.

Sometimes we're returned to winter
or winter just refuses to drive.

Sometimes I sing that song
from childhood and teach you

the words as you sleep. Sometimes
the neighborhood sparks loose

some change and we steal
the streets like they're ours to bend.

Sometimes it's yellow or sad, summer
flowers like equations beneath the rain.

Sometimes I, you. Sometimes nothing
turns the way our bodies do.

THE DOCTOR ASKS ME TO DESCRIBE THE PAIN

A kind of itch sinking beneath the water.
One eye slowly opening after surgery.
One punch to the chest. Everyone smiling.
Wax from a candle dripping to the thigh.
Happy Birthday sung through the trees as birds
taunt you in moonlight. Little coffin.
Little fingers. Green eyes squinting in the sun.
An electric cord bending back the bone.
The surgeon resting her head on your chest
and whispering *See you soon*. A kind of fever.
The body a kind of drowning. White dresses
fallen from a clothesline. A train window
slamming open, shut. Thirst of the chest.
Bird in the throat. A dog's blue growl.
The baby a kind of season. April, a kind
of stillness. Constellations shaped
like hammers. Hammers shaped like stars.

APOGEE

Rows of women
                    filled the hospital room,

green curtains our only   separation.

        We were there to wait,

tea and toast served to us

                    on trays, and still   we waited—

our stomachs betraying
                            our bodies, or

our bodies   betraying our babies.

        Hooked to machines, we silently

searched for signs   of movement, our babies

                    so quiet   we feared we may

never call their names,

                    each of us pretending   not to hear

the other's small   whispers, how

                            we cradled grief

on the edge of our tongues

        until only   the walls

                dared to answer.

SHOULD WE NEED TO ESCAPE

Walking through a front door left open
by a man we knew would not be home,

a radio in the kitchen murmured
through the hallway where we stood

waiting to be caught. We once imagined
being young meant forever

chasing the day we would no longer
harm ourselves, to speak to each other

in a language translated from our injuries.
From the entryway, unopened letters

lay visible across the dining room table.
We opened them because we could,

wanting to discover a woman as desperate
as we hoped to become, a car left running

in the driveway should we need to escape,
the house we found by following him

home from work urging us further inside.
We knew better than to seek out

the bedroom, too afraid to open a door
that might serve as a mirror of our lives—

an empty room save for the bed, a man awake
through the night, humming, reading, alone.

DAYTIME TELEVISION, LATE-NIGHT SEX

If this were a soap opera, the music would switch on
before we made it to the bed, the lights would dim

as if on cue: no need for knobs or remotes, electricity
would live only in the spaces where we touched.

On television, the hidden parts would be shown
in flashbacks between the sheets, our best angles

wrapping each other past spilled glasses of champagne,
lipstick newly applied, with a subtle coat and pair

of heels predictably sunk into the pink carpet
of a Paris hotel room. There would be no off-screen

shots of unwrapping condom, no clumsy reach for bra,
the long rip of a zipper, never in the back seat of a car

or up against a bathroom stall. We would wake
looking perfect, no worries except for what the writers

may throw our way: a sudden illness requiring a miracle
transplant, another woman who claims to be both my sister

and your ex-wife, the collapse of a cosmetics company
you inherited from your biological mother—or perhaps

a dead husband now alive, though the whole town
watched him fall from a bridge one year ago,

leaving nothing behind except my three-month pregnancy and a note telling me he's so sorry, and it's all my fault.

IN DOORWAYS, EVERY SIGN

Dear World: I'm trying to listen between
the voices. The geography grows its own accent

and this month it's not easy. We say love
in doorways, every sign above an entrance.

These places have known us, variations
of what we used to be. We say goodbye

as if to summarize the fragments between.
Or what. Or now. Or so. Or every bar

seems a signal, the distance a punch we shake.
The summer runs through the floor and color

cannot still the days. Watch me pull away
the red. Pretend I'm a flower crawling

over carpet. Mute the sound when I cry.
Dear World: I want to taste the miles between

everywhere and him. Oh please, I just want
to be hungry.

THE DOCTOR ASKS ME TO RECALL MY DREAM

My daughter lives long enough
to hand me a gift wrapped in muslin,

white fabric falling beside the bed.
Inside the box, six books form a circle,

spines shaped like the crust of a pie.
She tells me to close my eyes

and rips the pages before stacking them
in my hand, slices of words all that separate

my skin from hers. *Swallow this,* she whispers
before disappearing, small fingers

reaching inside my mouth
to place a paragraph on my tongue.

MESHES OF THE AFTERNOON

All invention and creation consists primarily of a new relationship between known parts.

—Maya Deren

It was twelve minutes

before the phone rang,
      the wind steering

each woman against afternoon.
      It was mirror at first

but soon a man, glass floating
      across bodies that were waves.

The key to the house now housed
      above tongue—or so the voice

on the record sings, each ring
      of the phone a silent scene

spoken through walls.
      She is sandal, is flash,

is sleep, is knife, water
      burying staircase and throat.

It was flower but then noon,
      the loaf of bread

lost to field,
        every mouth unhooked,

calling.

DEAR HANDS,

I cannot wake up. Some nights, a green porch
is all that's left, rain dripping through blue lights.
Everywhere, a new name. Dear Hotel, I cannot

unhinge the hour. The streets are without bridges,
the ceiling without stars. We moved against.
We touched beside. Some nights, he's gone, still

circling the river where once we kissed, crawled,
were through with the other. Dear January, some say
we swallowed winter, held our bodies in snow.

Dear Envelope, it was the neck's only migration.
Some nights, insects crash through the window
and we're closer to sky again, colorless currents.

Dear Cities, I cannot trace the edges. Dear
Leaves, I cannot recall the red. Dear Broken,
Dear Near, Dear Always, Dear Nothing—I cannot.

BLUE FEATHERS

I dream the birds nesting outside the house
fly to the hospital to see me, blue feathers
falling to my chest. I am never alone

and yet the birds call as if they mean
to speak to only me, and not to her.
They perch by my ear and whisper

We can save her, but we won't.

DOMICILE

THE FUNERAL YEAR

I built a headstone from baby blocks,
tiny letters stacked across the bed.

Flowers crept through cracks in the floorboard,
a procession of words caught under my tongue,

strange names for rain, sun.
I spoke to weather but not to myself.

I reached for the glass. I hid behind stone.
I spelled her portrait across my body,

skirted the lines between limb and vein
until even the idea of her felt cool to the touch.

I planned my own funeral instead of hers,
the map to the house swallowed through clouds.

And still, doctors gathered outside my window,
a nest of eggs buried beneath their feet.

LIBRARIES

How the room is like a library, grief
collected each night as she falls.

How she stumbles across the steps
of the library, pages of glass

buried in her skin. The library
is where he removes the glass

then leaves his hands like a page
unturned on her thigh.

How the doctors move like a library,
the unread sentences a red

awakening placed on reserve.
A library drowns the monuments

she sees each night before sleep.
A library pinches the arm,

her nerves encased through glass.
How she buries him in the arm,

the disease of the library
blistered, restless. How she plans

the funeral in a library, every book
a litany of urges to borrow and return.

EACH MORNING, I WAKE REACHING

And suddenly, I itch in my sleep. Bees
land on my arms until their stingers
are a cloud pressing on my chest,
the doctor's question rolling
across the floor like a ball
left in the yard—

                              What is this?

What is this?

The porcelain doll I found
in the water keeps returning
to sit in a chair by the window.
Birds squeeze through cracks
in the glass, their eyes stitched shut
as they hover above the bed.

I no longer look away.

Each morning, I wake reaching
for my feet, the grip of rats
running loose over the sheets.

This is how I know she is still with me.

32 WEEKS

Still dark, I listen for the flap
of wings as I walk beside the river.

Before I was sick, before the doctors
said my body would not sustain hers,

I sat each afternoon on the hill
behind the cathedral, a foal napping

in the field as anchored narrowboats
quietly shifted close to shore.

It went on like this until one day
the foal was gone, its mother

standing alone beneath the trees
as I walked to the hospital in the rain.

Now I walk until the birds
land beside me, their blue wings wet

where the river skims the path.

YEARS FROM NOW, I REMEMBER OUR VACATION

Tell me about the time she was sixteen
and the three of us swam in the ocean.

Tell me how it felt when the drugs pulled her
from water, the same dream split against

the window, the root. The clock spells noon
and the kitchen reads warm, which means

we're together again, which means you thought
you saw her last night in the street.

So what if the fruit is burning.
So what if the stove burns my thumb.

Tell me the doctors are wrong. Tell me
about the dream where my daughter grows old.

34 WEEKS

The waiting was like a dance
inside me, a gunshot fired
across a clear field

I remembered walking past
years before I knew
she may leave me.

It was easier to imagine her
standing on a platform
as a train approached,

the blame I placed
everywhere except myself
only a whisper of an engine

still not born, the doctors
standing on the track
warning *Too late, too late.*

THE DOCTOR ASKS ME TO IMAGINE MY BABY ALIVE

And then one day, the birds
were gone.

Behind the house, their feathers
        sank beneath the water

so fast it seemed they forgot
their promise to take her,

      cracked eggs by the door
all that remained.

IN MY DREAM, I ALWAYS REMEMBER THE NAMES OF TREES

She walks beside me, the crabgrass high
around our ankles. Clouds hum
above our heads, the color of the sky

a river we swim through before reaching
a field of brambles. I squeeze the berries

into a glass and she turns her back
as I take a sip. Perhaps it is better this way,
her face hidden as I place my hand on her back.

I ask no questions. If she leaves again,
it will be before I've spoken.

Heat rose from machines. The doctors
said to keep walking and so I did, climbing
the same stairwell for hours at a time.

The baby no longer moving, I continued
to pace the hallways as evening approached.
It seemed to move was a theme

I could not escape that year, two countries
defined by what was missing, the same way
I once woke from surgery and knew

where I was only by asking where I was not.
It wasn't until I was still that I felt
the baby was coming, the draft

from the window steadying my balance
as my husband stopped and whispered
Do you want to turn back?

LETTING THE BODY DECIDE

She turns as I sleep, arms
trembling in colors blue and wide,

bones that drift beneath stars, snow.
Consider the dream: a river

mapped from one leg to the next.
Consider the mouth: fields frozen

beyond the window of a train.
I call her Juniper. I call for help.

The weather pushes against us.
Ice climbs through branches

and streets no longer wake.
Consider her born.

Consider each river a name.
Consider the mornings I walked

the path alone. My body,
her captor—and somewhere,

the fog rising, the ground
refusing to let us go.

SAY THE EELS RETURN

I want to wake and find every boat unlatched,

see each brick painted white.

I want no bells to ring.

I want the promise of hills. Clouds.

Every name written on the backs of our knees.

I want the eels to return to the river.

I want to hear you say they never left,

that our hands won't remember,

that it's true across the tracks,

in the roof of the mouth,

what the doctors say.

I want to be a slip of shadow rising,

the proper spelling for the body of the sun.

I want a moon frozen in daylight.

I want to know it's summer, somewhere—

TO BRING MILK ANYWAY

It seemed cruel of the body
to bring milk anyway,
having been told the baby

may not survive.
But still, my breasts grew
heavy from the cries of children

not my own. What use
do we have for the stars on nights
the ocean can't be heard?

For a few hours, I let the milk
gather beneath my shirt
as I sat by the window, the sky

a ledge from which I imagined
others jumped.

AN ARCHAEOLOGY

A flood moves slower than history
ever shows, our bodies already

artifacts of the grass, clouds
buried beside the trees

like letters we carve through snow.
We survey words around us.

Stone begins to crack in each step
and we carry the pieces behind the house.

Doctors climb inside me, an excavation
to map where a baby once grew.

I draw pictures of where I sleep
and still you always find me awake.

They say even weather eventually sleeps.
They say even centuries keep vigil.

They say even we were once a city:
two halves parted by a river,

the remains of what we were
lost in the landslide

of what we became.

CHERRY HILL

I stood with my back to the cathedral,
the streets of the town no busier
than before. Narrowboats lined the river
where branches swept the water,
the house where we first lived
steps from the path of the flood.
From the top window, I used to listen
for the call of the trains,
the baby we had just brought home
sleeping in our bed—and somewhere
beyond the tracks, an ocean between
then and now, a circle of rain rising.

There were bridges all around us.
No hills that we could see.
A house with windows
we swung outward to open.
Cracks in the paint that meant
mold crept through our lungs.
We walked the ruins of an abbey,
stone chipped to arrows
like fingers pointing skyward.
We secured bookcases to the walls.
We scrubbed the back of furniture.
Further into town, eels slept
in small tanks beside market stalls.
It always rained, but lightning
never appeared. We stacked
our boots beside the staircase.
Closed every door to trap the heat.
A train came daily across the river
but the city seemed far away.
We carried groceries through wind,
snow. Always discounted bread
by afternoon. Each spring, horses
slept in fields behind the cathedral.
If we knew one day all of this would live
only in our bones, we never let on.
We measured time by how long
we were together, never by counting
the days until we were gone.

WATERSIDE

Boats lined the river that summer—
hottest on record—parked in perfect

rows outside our favorite pub.
The baby slept against my chest

as we sat in the grass, the park
cooler than our bedroom,

dishes clicking against shelves
from an evening's open window.

Men sat in chairs on top of their boats,
each roof casting a shadow

along the path to the station.
The trains moved in silence

across the river, only the baby stirring
as lights from passenger windows

flickered across the water.
I listened to the bells ringing

from the cathedral as the baby's
mouth brushed my neck,

tapping the hours with my palm
the way the machines in the hospital

once traced her heartbeat,
her lips so warm I almost forgot

how she was nearly not here
until she was.

NOTES

Many of the poems in the book describe or make reference to intra-hepatic cholestasis of pregnancy (ICP), a liver condition that occurs in pregnancy and causes severe itching in the mother—particularly in the hands and feet—as well as increasing the risk of prematurity, fetal distress, and stillbirth.

"Cut" is after Alison Stine's poem "Gossip."

"Meshes of the Afternoon" shares a title with and is inspired by the 1943 short experimental film *Meshes of the Afternoon*, directed by Maya Deren and Alexander Hammid.

"Blue Feathers" takes its title from a line in Allison Seay's poem "Bathing."

"Letting the Body Decide" takes its title from Deniz Peters' paper "Letting the Body Decide: Creativity, Gesture and Musical Embodiment in Space as a Virtual Instrument," which was presented at the CMPCP Performance Studies Network International Conference at the University of Cambridge in July 2011.